Charge into Reading

Decodable Reader
with literacy activities

Grub Grab
R Blends

Brooke Vitale • Mila Uvarova

CHARGE MOMMY
BOOKS
Riverside, CT

Copyright © 2023 Charge Mommy Books, LLC. All rights reserved.

No part of this book may be reproduced or transmitted in any form or by any means, electronic or mechanical, including photocopying, recording, or by any information storage and retrieval system, without written permission from the publisher.

For information address contact@chargemommybooks.com
or visit chargemommybooks.com

Library of Congress Control Number: 2023904016

Printed in China
ISBN 978-1-955947-32-9
10 9 8 7 6

Designed by Lindsay Broderick
Created in consultation with literacy specialist Marisa Ware, MSEd

Grant grabs a box.
Grant preps the box.

Brad grabs the grub.
He drops the grub in the box.

Grant grabs six grubs.
He crams the grubs in the box.

A frog hops past Grant.

Grant grabs the frog.

Grant grins.
"I got the frog," Grant brags.

Grant grips the frog.
He trots to the box.

Grant trips.

Drat!
Grant drops the frog.

Grant frets.
The frog is brisk!

Brad traps the frog in the box.
"Got it," Brad brags.

Grant tips the lid.
He gasps.

The frog fed on the grubs! Brad!

Let's Talk Literacy!

Read the sentence below. Then circle the picture that matches the sentence.

Grant grips the frog.

Let's Talk Literacy!

Each of the words below begins with an R blend. Sound out each word. Then draw a line from **each word** to its **matching picture**.

crab drop drum frog grub print

  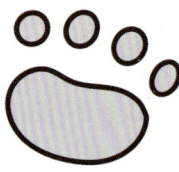

Let's Talk Literacy!

Say the name of each picture below. Then circle the words that begin with an **R blend**.

Answers: grapes, crayons, brush, pretzel

Let's Talk Literacy!

Read each word below. Then circle the pictures in each row that have names beginning with the same **initial consonant blend**.

crib

grab

trot

Answers: crown, crayons / grub, grass, grapes / tree, truck, triangle

Let's Talk Literacy!

Say the name of each picture below. Then circle the correct **initial consonant blend** for each word.

Answers: frog, tree, brush, bread, crab, drum

Let's Talk Literacy!

Write the letters that form each picture word in the boxes below. Then draw a **scoop mark** under each consonant blend.

Answers: f-r-o-g / c-r-a-b / d-r-u-m

Let's Talk Literacy!

The name of each picture below begins with a different consonant blend. Sort the words in the **word bank** by putting them under the picture of the word that uses the **same consonant blend**.

brag   crisp   prop   grunt
brim   grin   crop   prep

Let's Talk Literacy!

Say the name of each picture below. Then write the word's **initial consonant blend** on the line below the picture. The first one has been done for you.

gr _____ _____ _____ _____

  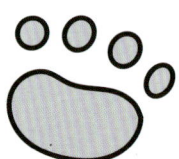 

_____ _____ _____ _____

Answers: grill, crayons, tree, drill, brick, dress, print, truck